ALPHA '16

CHELSEA MILES

ENFIELD ~ CONNECTICUT

Afroed Dizzy Yak

Bristol

Crispybones

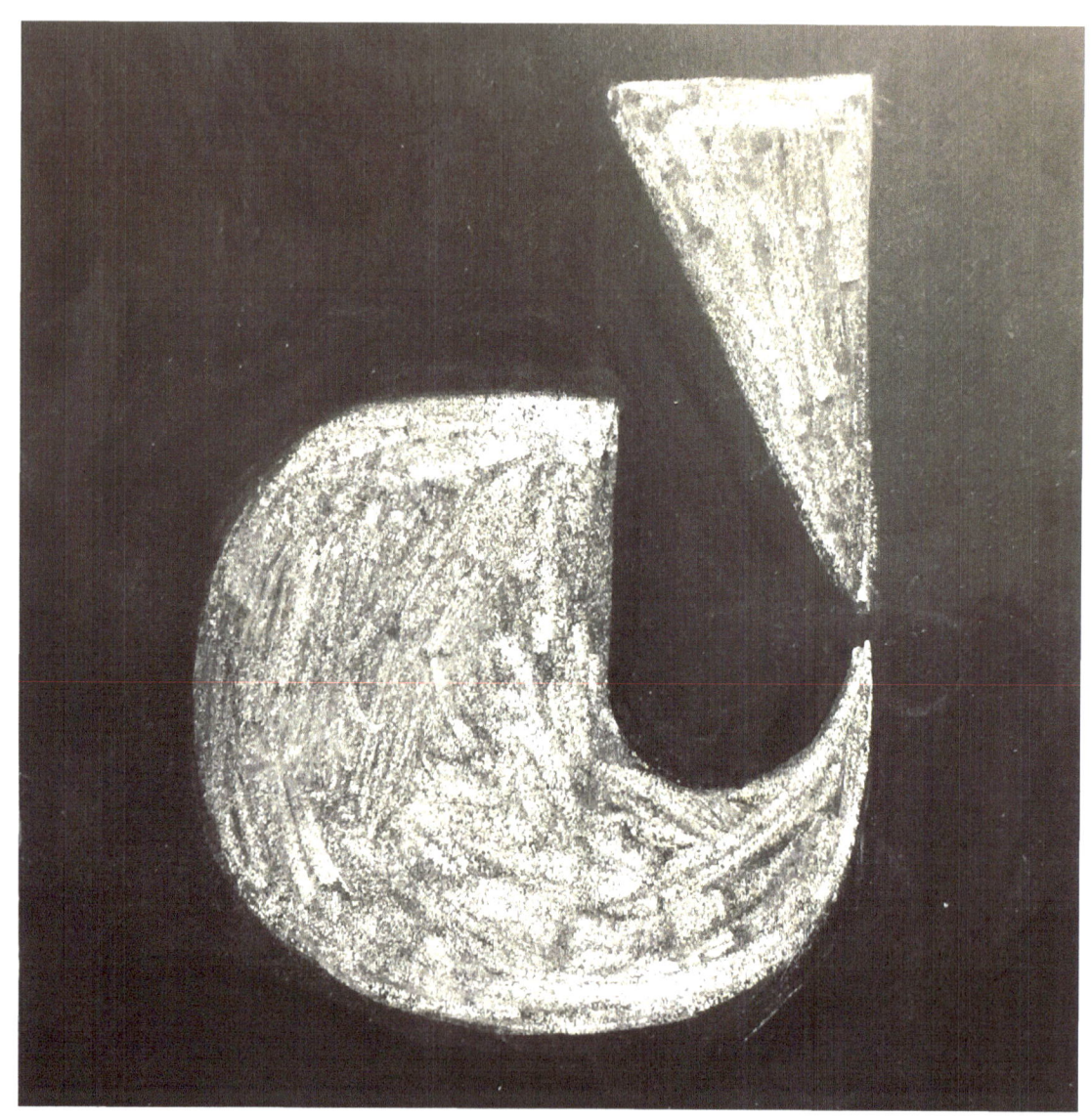

Da Sei Nei

Showtime

Steiner

Ergono

Spicy Rice

Bellbottom

Ice Cream Soda

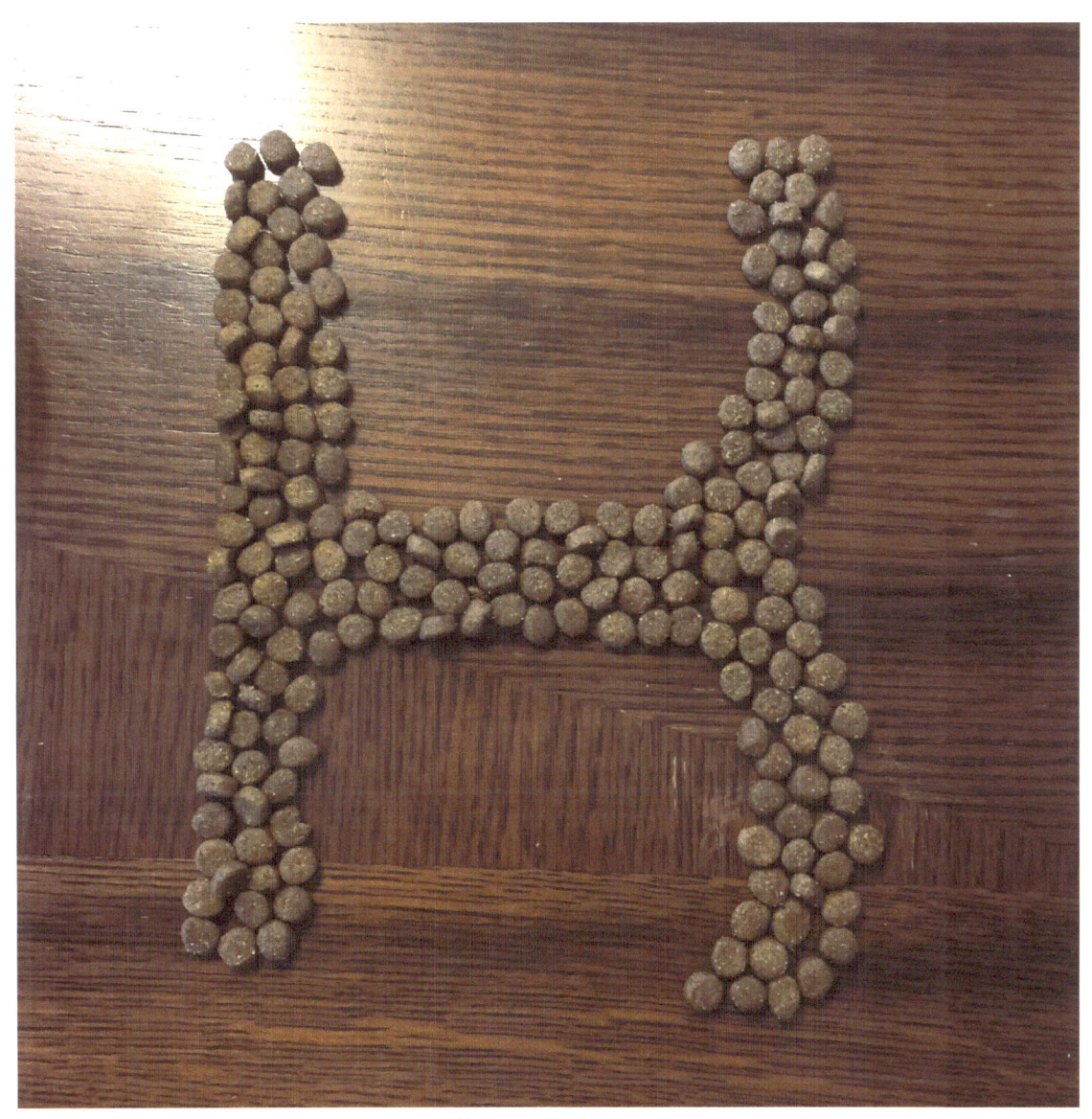

Goca Logo

Limelight Regular

Mandela Script

Coraline's Cat

Retro

Plicata

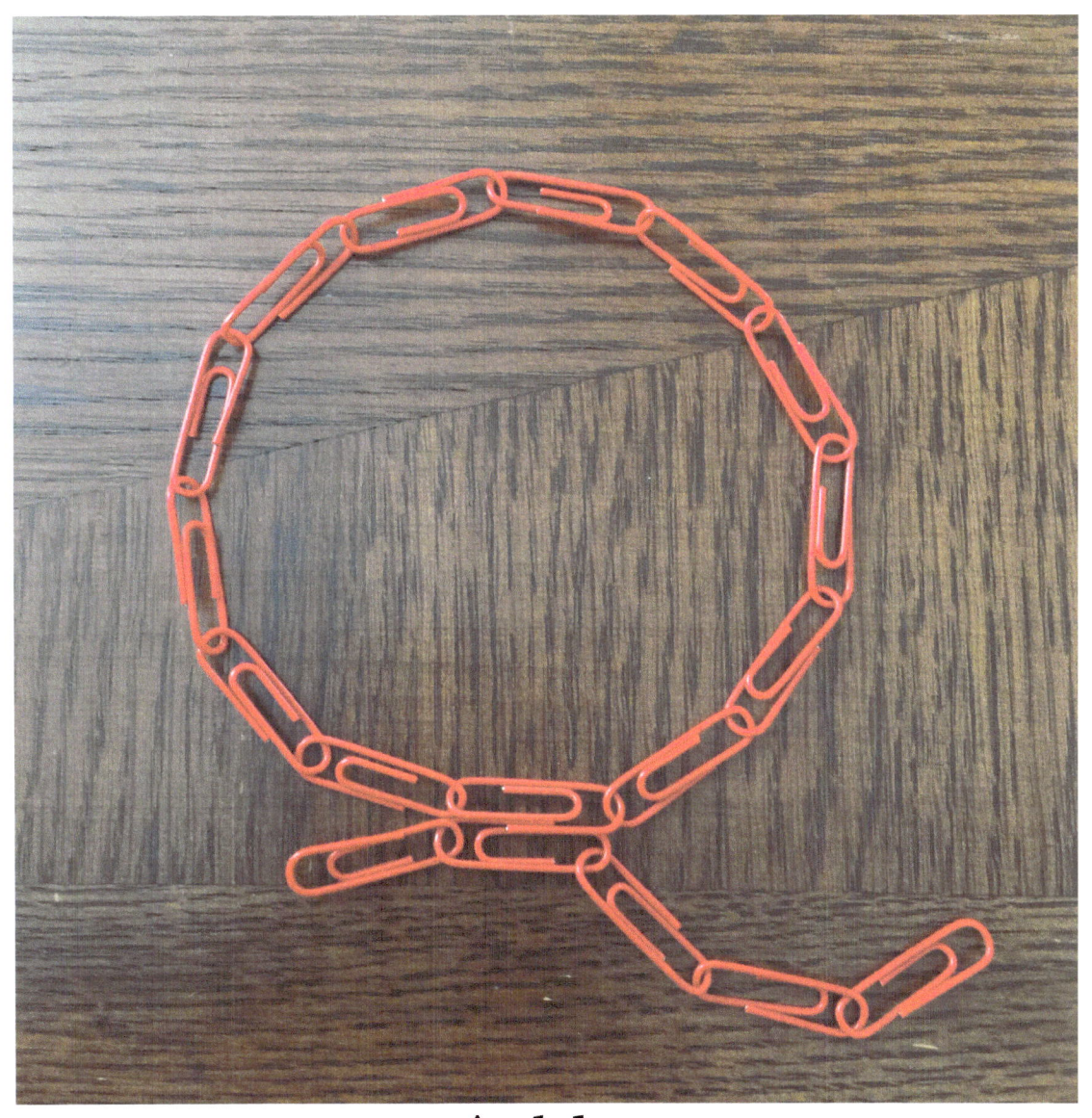

Andalus

Miog

Minimal

Times New Roman

Morden

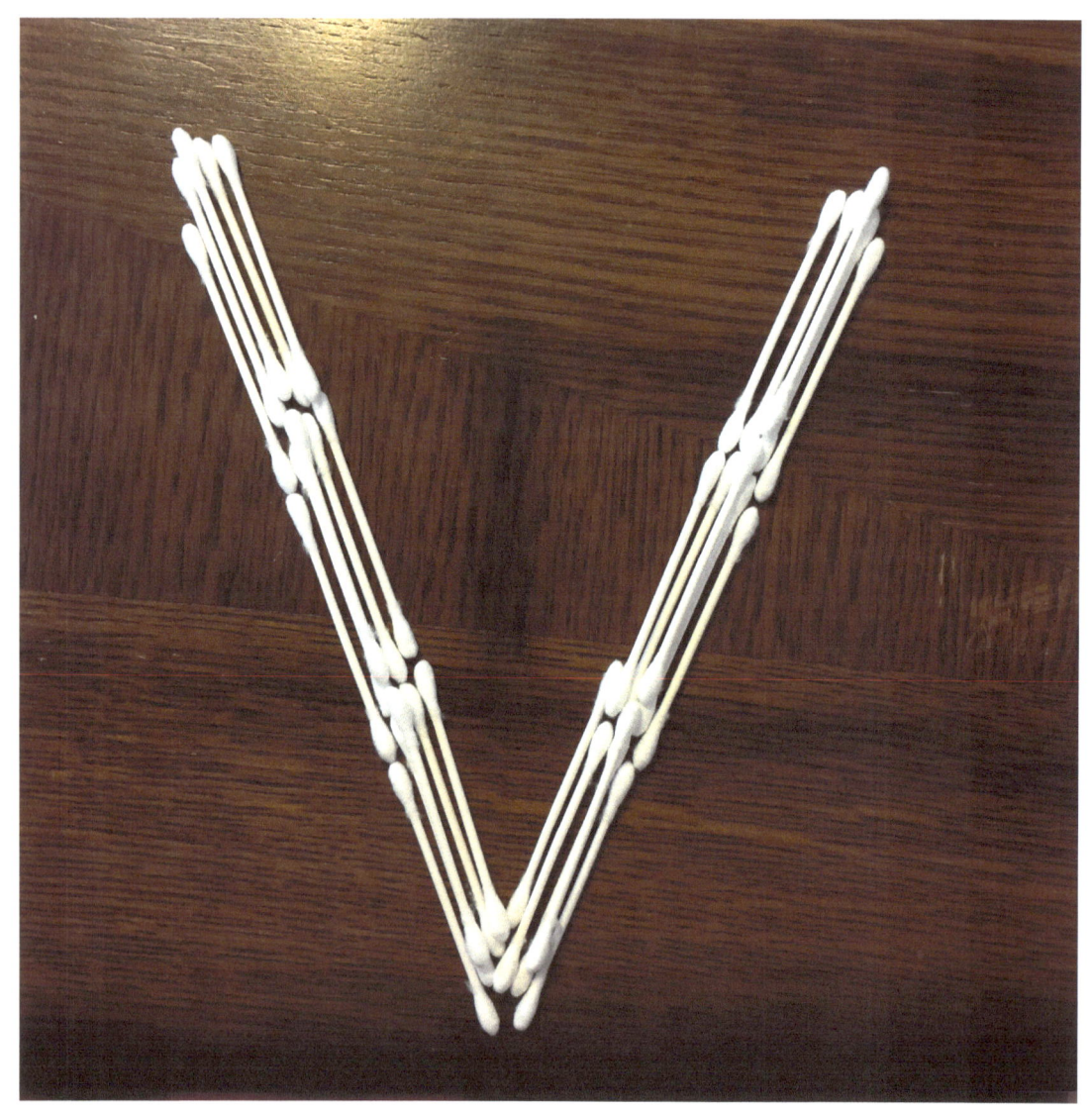

Verdana

Lucida Handwriting

Mers

Comic Sans

Mooglonk

Magnolia

Mayton

MCM

Tekton Pro

Baskerville

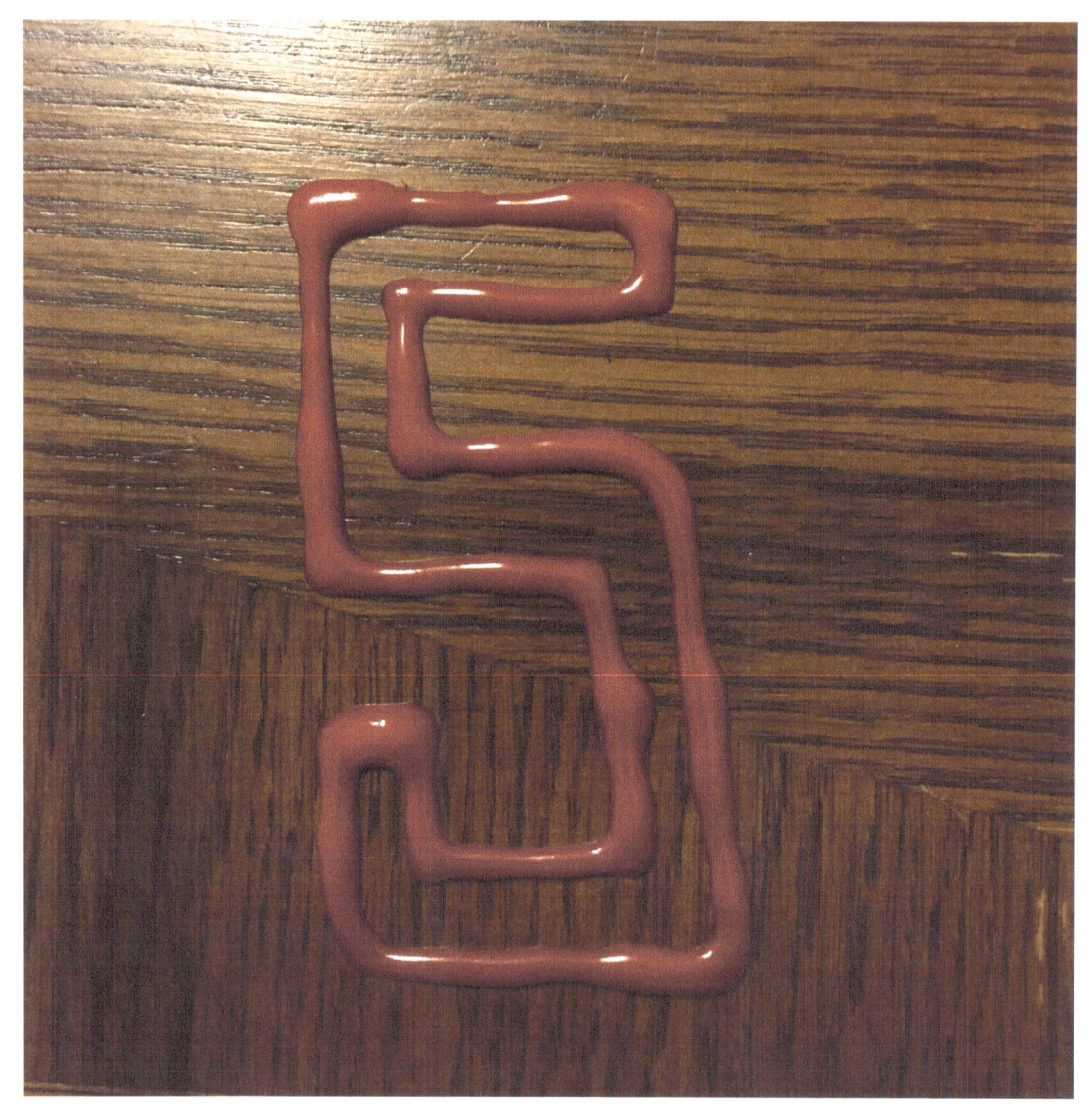

Agency Font Bold

Brush Script

Garamond

Bauhaus

Jokerman

Fin.

www.ingramcontent.com/pod-product-compliance
Lightning Source LLC
Chambersburg PA
CBHW060838290526
45792CB00006BB/1978